My First
HUMAN BODY BOOK

Donald M. Silver & Patricia J. Wynne

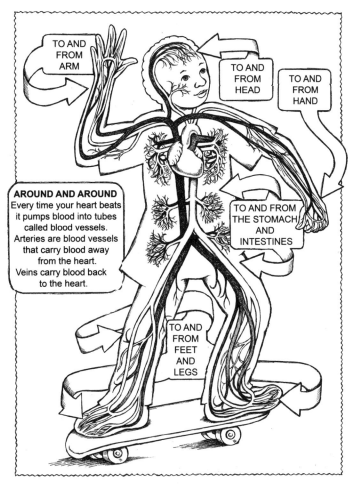

TO AND FROM ARM

TO AND FROM HEAD

TO AND FROM HAND

AROUND AND AROUND
Every time your heart beats it pumps blood into tubes called blood vessels. Arteries are blood vessels that carry blood away from the heart. Veins carry blood back to the heart.

TO AND FROM THE STOMACH AND INTESTINES

TO AND FROM FEET AND LEGS

DOVER PUBLICATIONS, INC.
Mineola, New York

Note

What is a hiccup? Where is my DNA? What does my skin do? These mysteries of the human body and many more are revealed in pictures and print in this amazing coloring book featuring the muscular, skeletal, nervous, digestive, respiratory, and immune systems. Easy-to-understand captions explain how we eat and breathe, move our bones, pump blood, and much more. All of the illustrations are in full detail with descriptions of every element involved. Have fun coloring the pictures with crayons, pencils, or markers as you learn about all the different body functions.

Bibliographical Note

My First Human Body Book is a new work, first published by
Dover Publications, Inc., in 2009.

International Standard Book Number

ISBN-13: 978-0-486-46821-1
ISBN-10: 0-486-46821-6

Manufactured in the United States by LSC Communications
46821613   2017
www.doverpublications.com

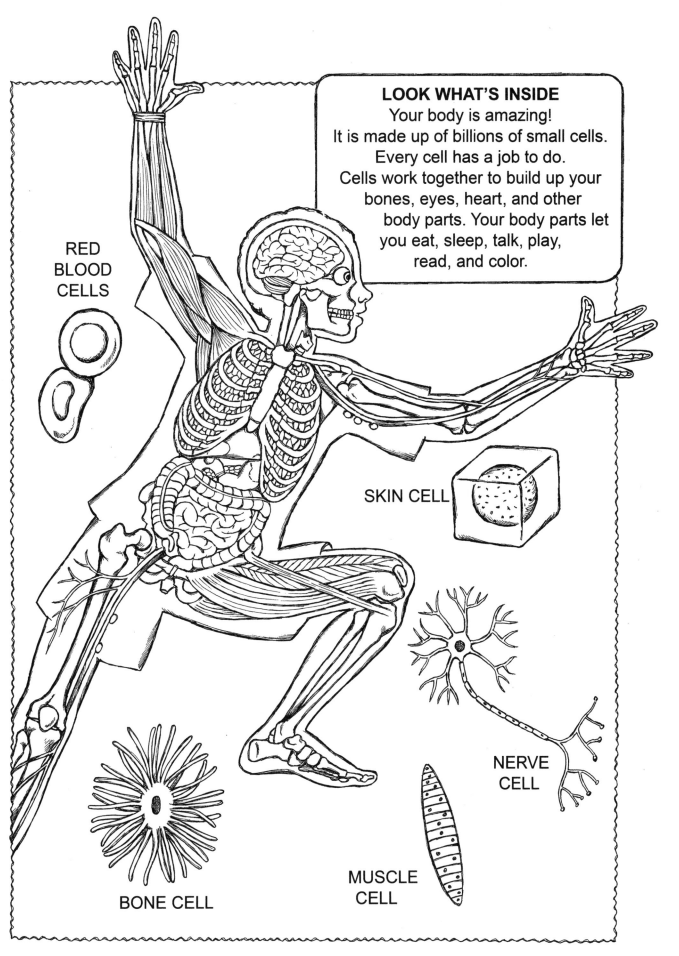

LOOK WHAT'S INSIDE
Your body is amazing!
It is made up of billions of small cells.
Every cell has a job to do.
Cells work together to build up your
bones, eyes, heart, and other
body parts. Your body parts let
you eat, sleep, talk, play,
read, and color.

RED
BLOOD
CELLS

SKIN CELL

NERVE
CELL

BONE CELL

MUSCLE
CELL

1

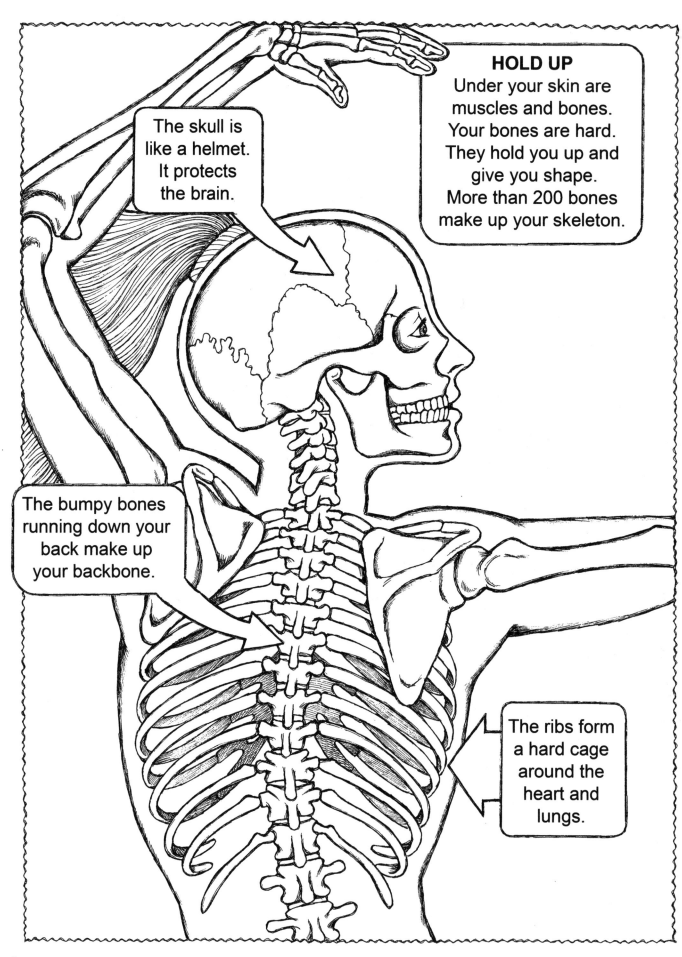

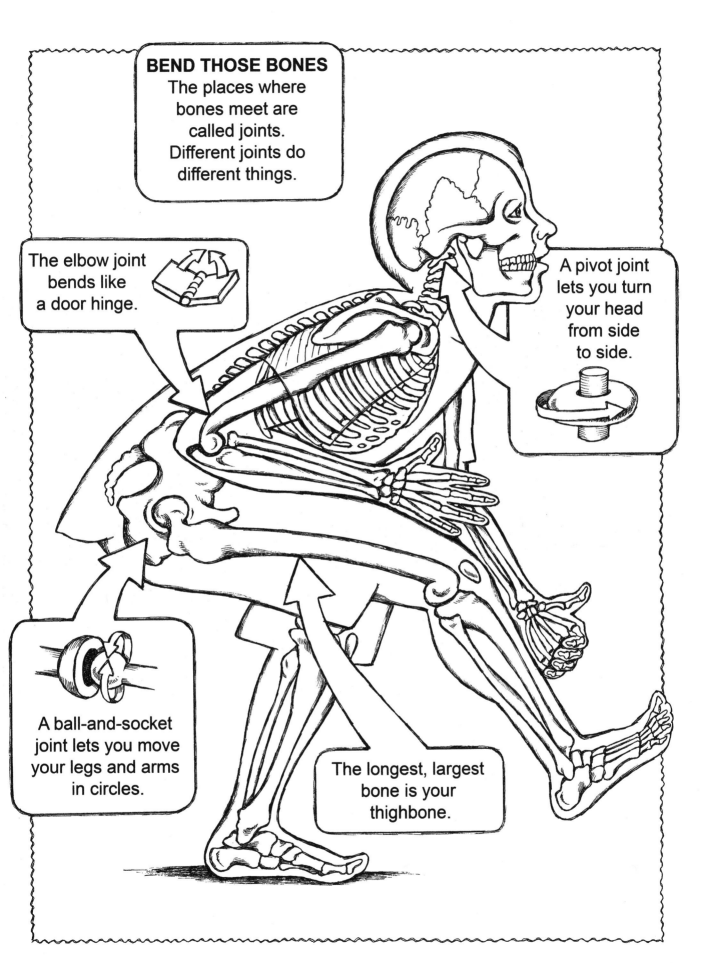

BEND THOSE BONES
The places where bones meet are called joints. Different joints do different things.

The elbow joint bends like a door hinge.

A pivot joint lets you turn your head from side to side.

A ball-and-socket joint lets you move your legs and arms in circles.

The longest, largest bone is your thighbone.

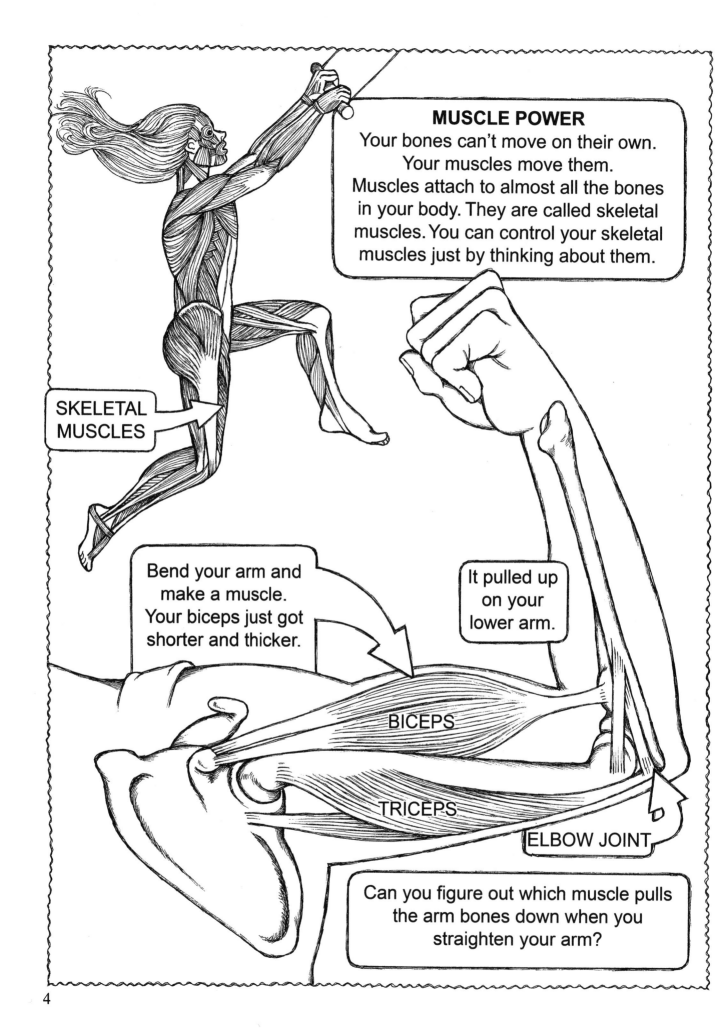

4

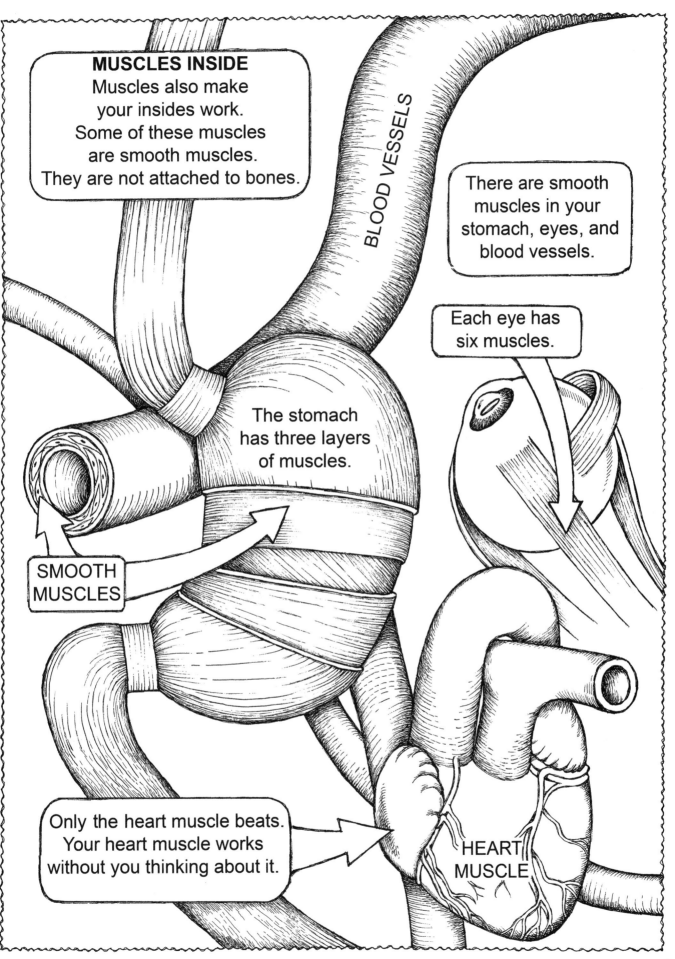

5

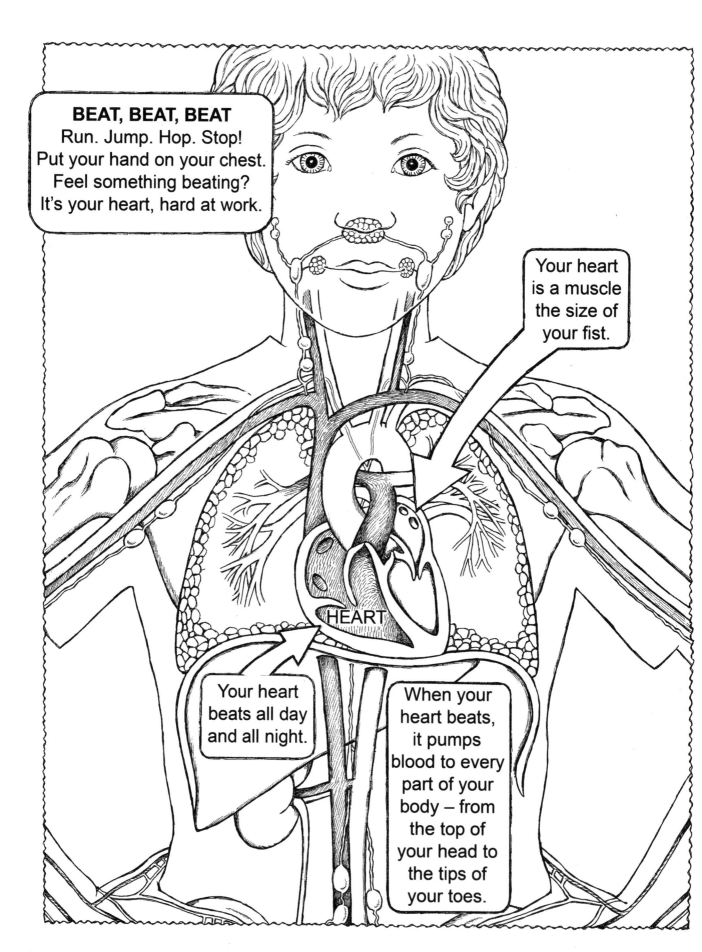

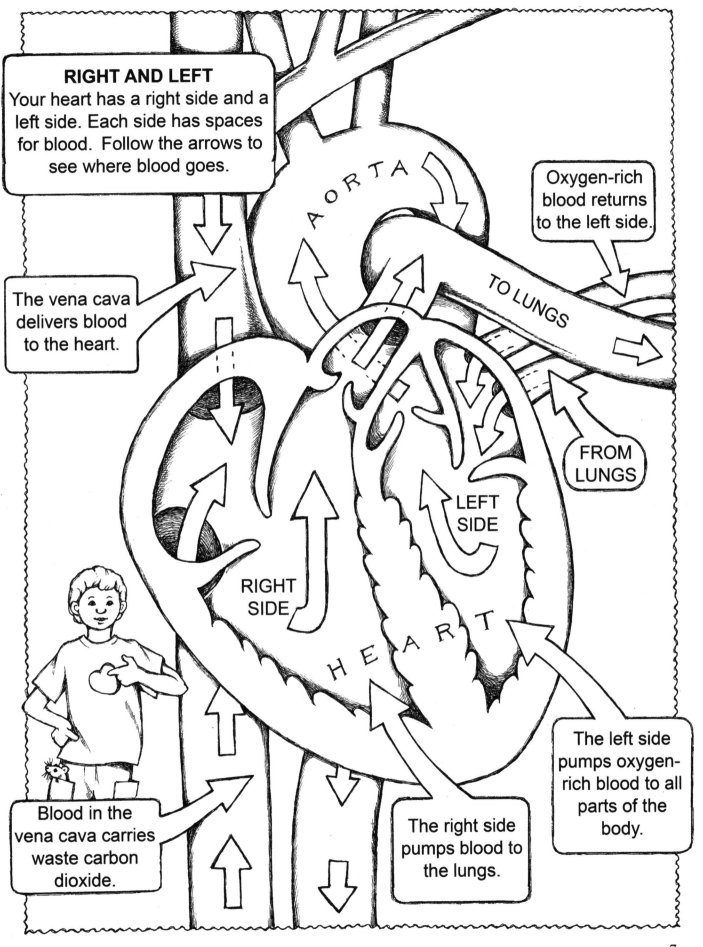

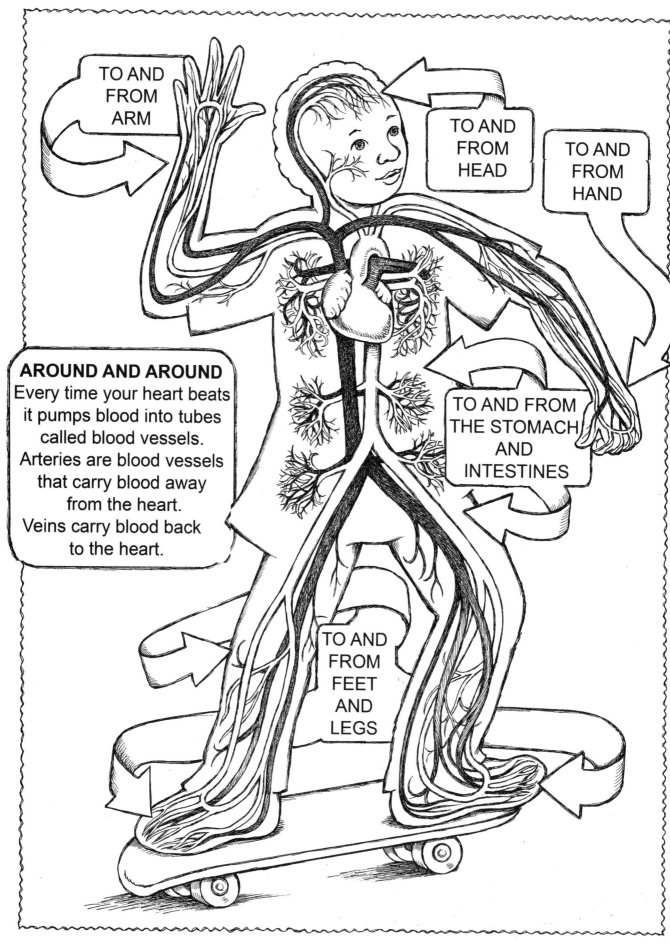

TO AND FROM ARM

TO AND FROM HEAD

TO AND FROM HAND

AROUND AND AROUND
Every time your heart beats it pumps blood into tubes called blood vessels. Arteries are blood vessels that carry blood away from the heart. Veins carry blood back to the heart.

TO AND FROM THE STOMACH AND INTESTINES

TO AND FROM FEET AND LEGS

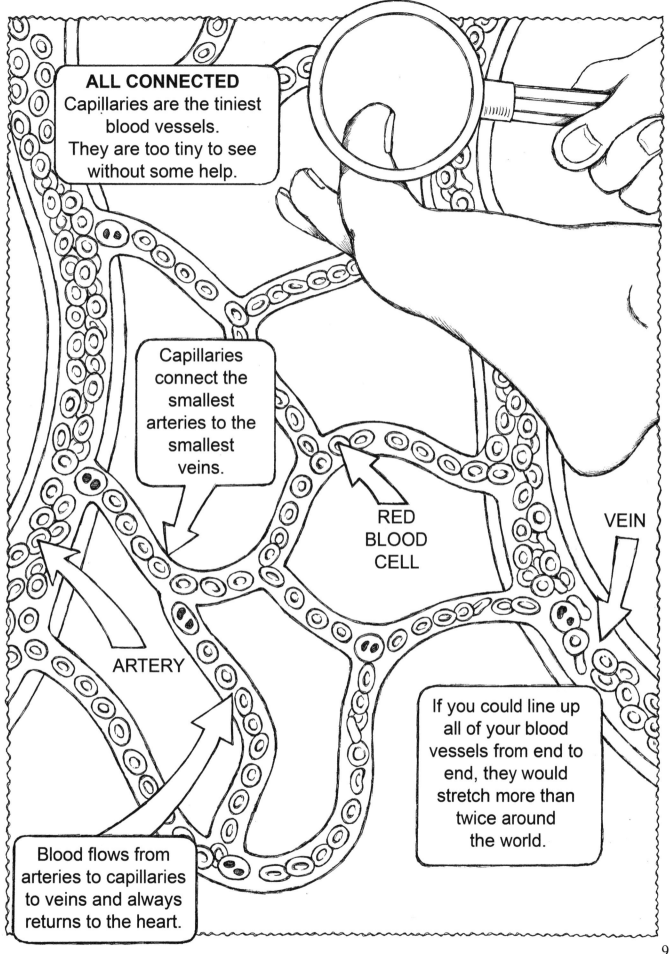

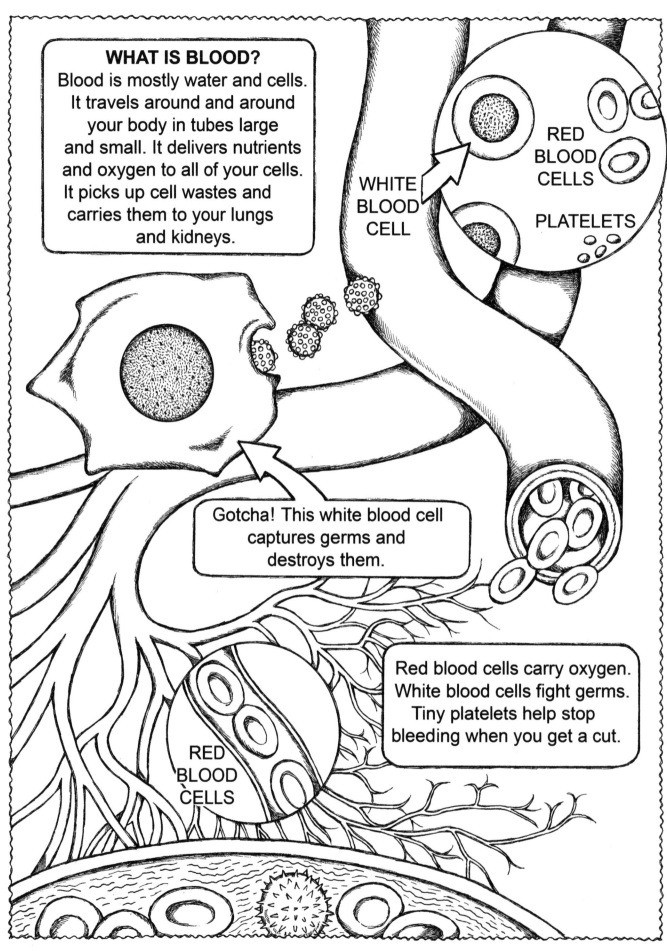

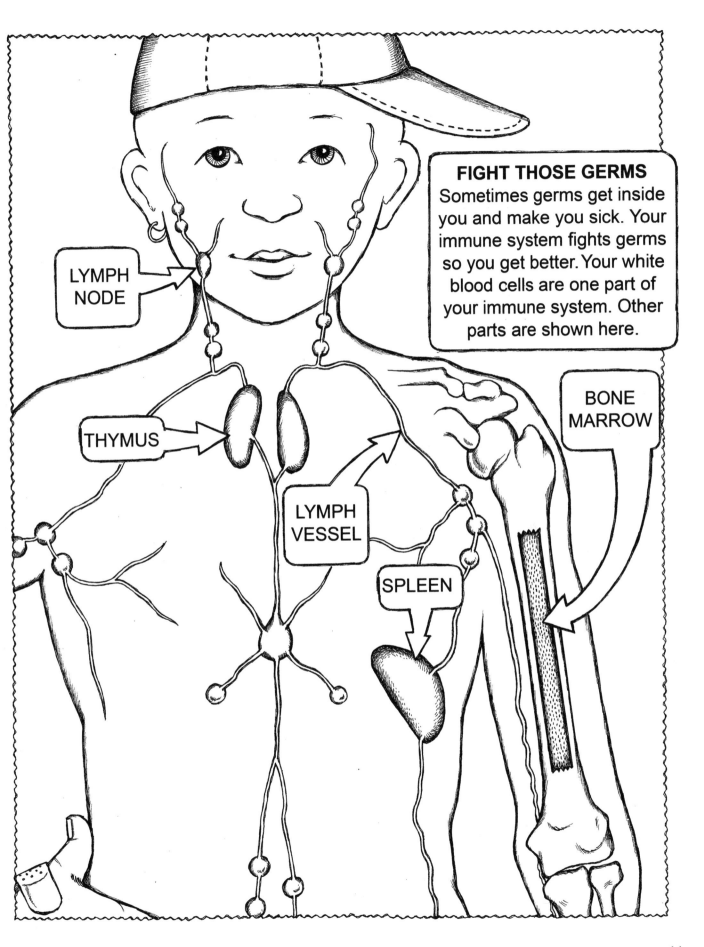

LYMPH NODE

FIGHT THOSE GERMS
Sometimes germs get inside you and make you sick. Your immune system fights germs so you get better. Your white blood cells are one part of your immune system. Other parts are shown here.

BONE MARROW

THYMUS

LYMPH VESSEL

SPLEEN

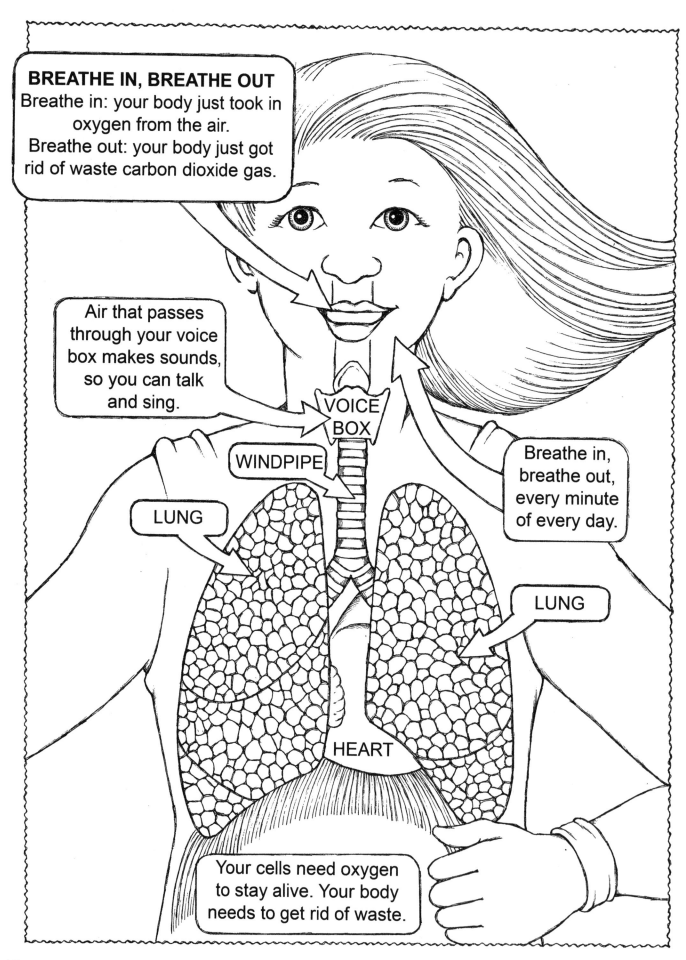

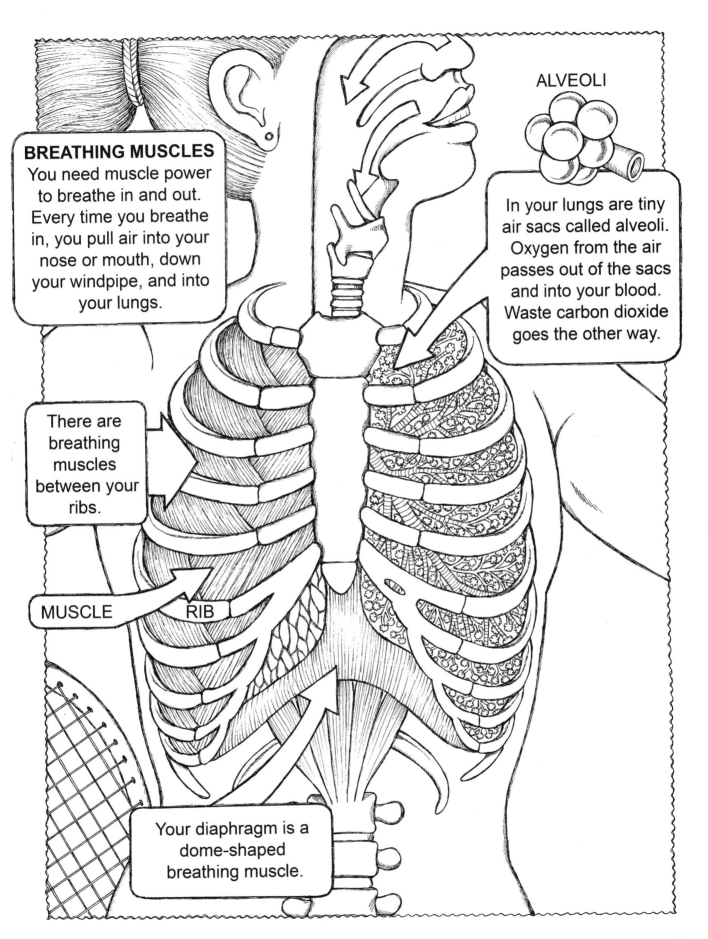

BREATHING MUSCLES
You need muscle power to breathe in and out. Every time you breathe in, you pull air into your nose or mouth, down your windpipe, and into your lungs.

ALVEOLI

In your lungs are tiny air sacs called alveoli. Oxygen from the air passes out of the sacs and into your blood. Waste carbon dioxide goes the other way.

There are breathing muscles between your ribs.

MUSCLE

RIB

Your diaphragm is a dome-shaped breathing muscle.

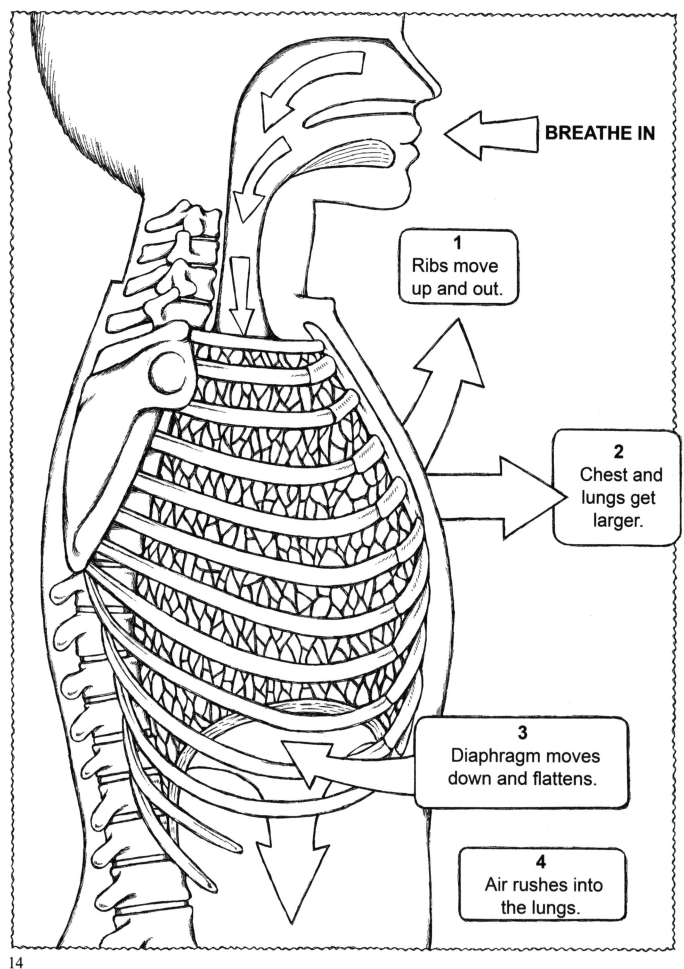

BREATHE IN

1
Ribs move
up and out.

2
Chest and
lungs get
larger.

3
Diaphragm moves
down and flattens.

4
Air rushes into
the lungs.

14

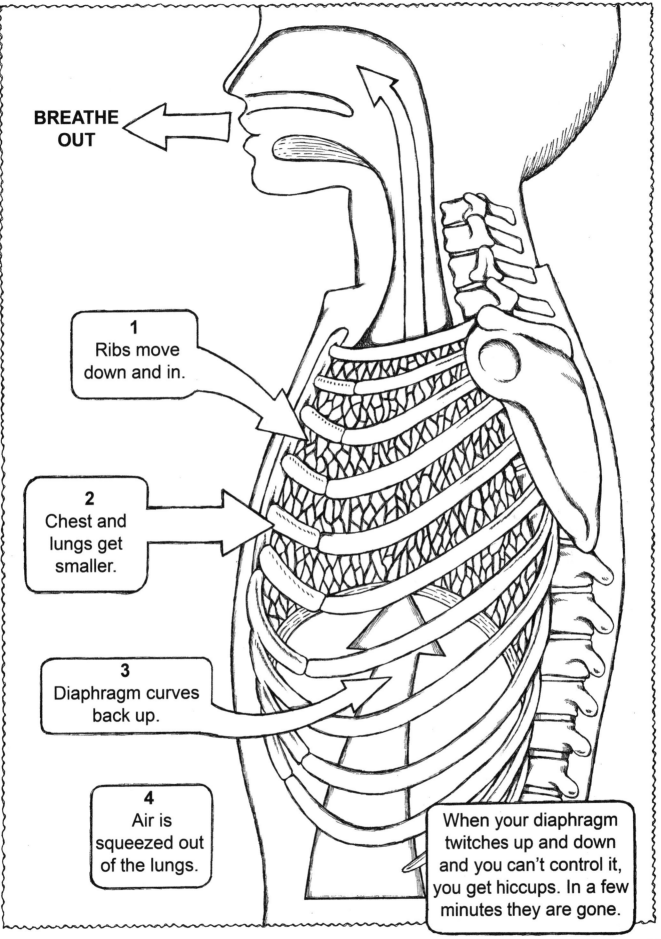

BREATHE OUT

1
Ribs move down and in.

2
Chest and lungs get smaller.

3
Diaphragm curves back up.

4
Air is squeezed out of the lungs.

When your diaphragm twitches up and down and you can't control it, you get hiccups. In a few minutes they are gone.

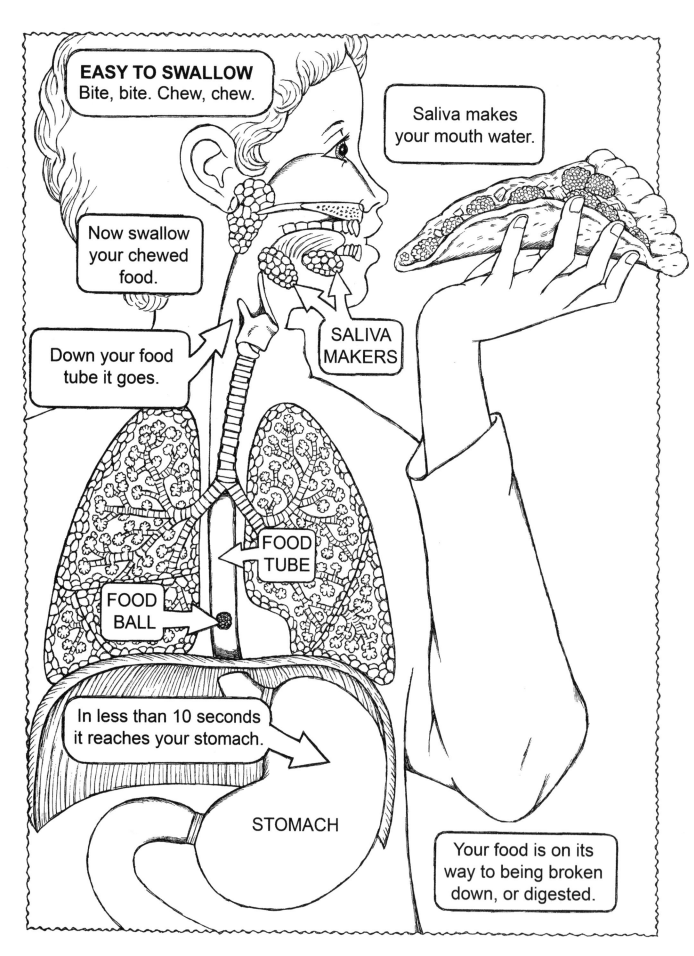

16

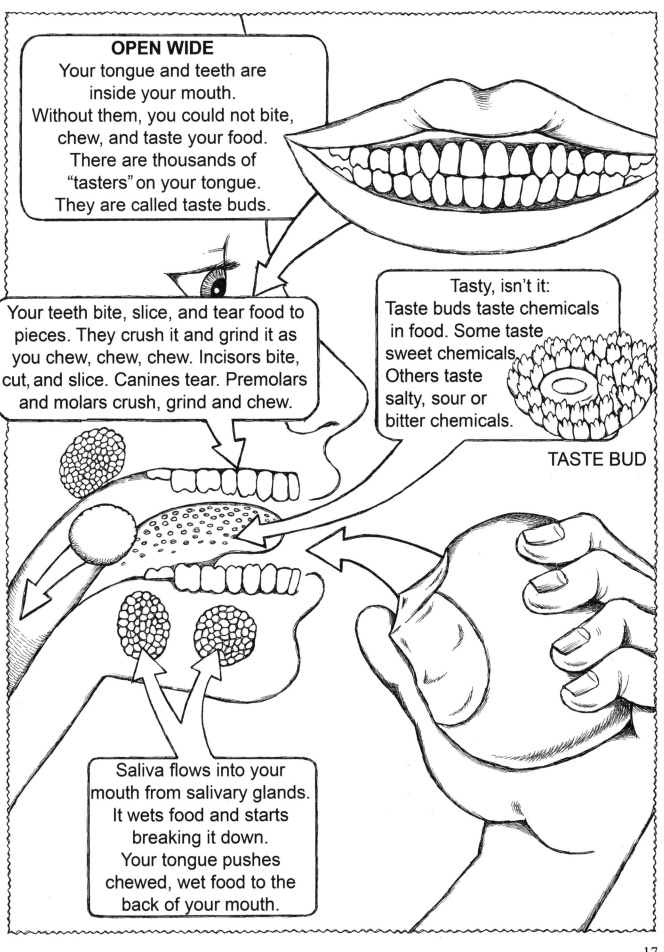

OPEN WIDE
Your tongue and teeth are inside your mouth. Without them, you could not bite, chew, and taste your food. There are thousands of "tasters" on your tongue. They are called taste buds.

Your teeth bite, slice, and tear food to pieces. They crush it and grind it as you chew, chew, chew. Incisors bite, cut, and slice. Canines tear. Premolars and molars crush, grind and chew.

Tasty, isn't it: Taste buds taste chemicals in food. Some taste sweet chemicals. Others taste salty, sour or bitter chemicals.

TASTE BUD

Saliva flows into your mouth from salivary glands. It wets food and starts breaking it down. Your tongue pushes chewed, wet food to the back of your mouth.

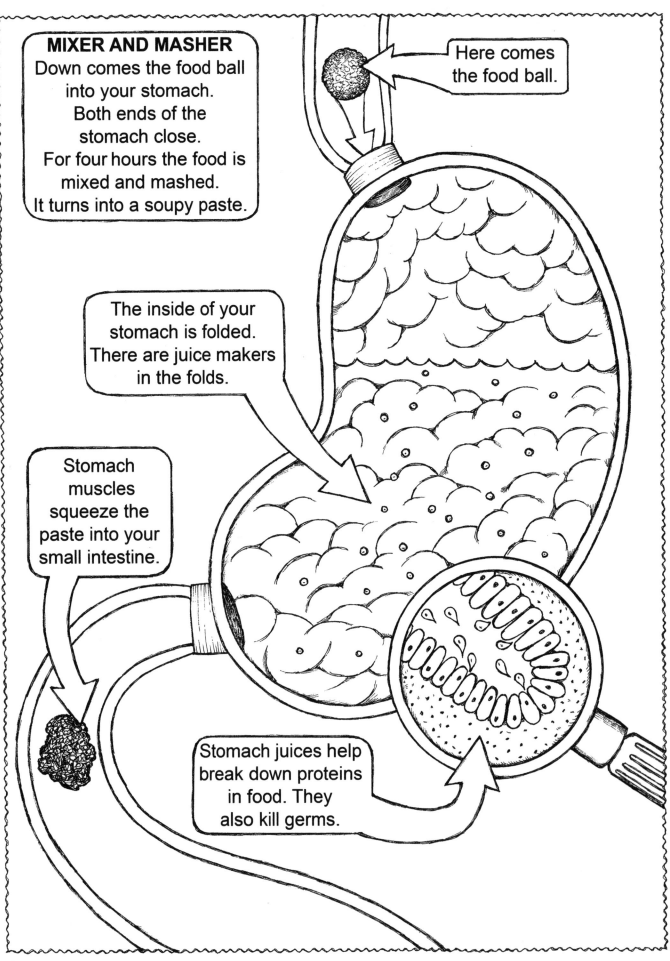

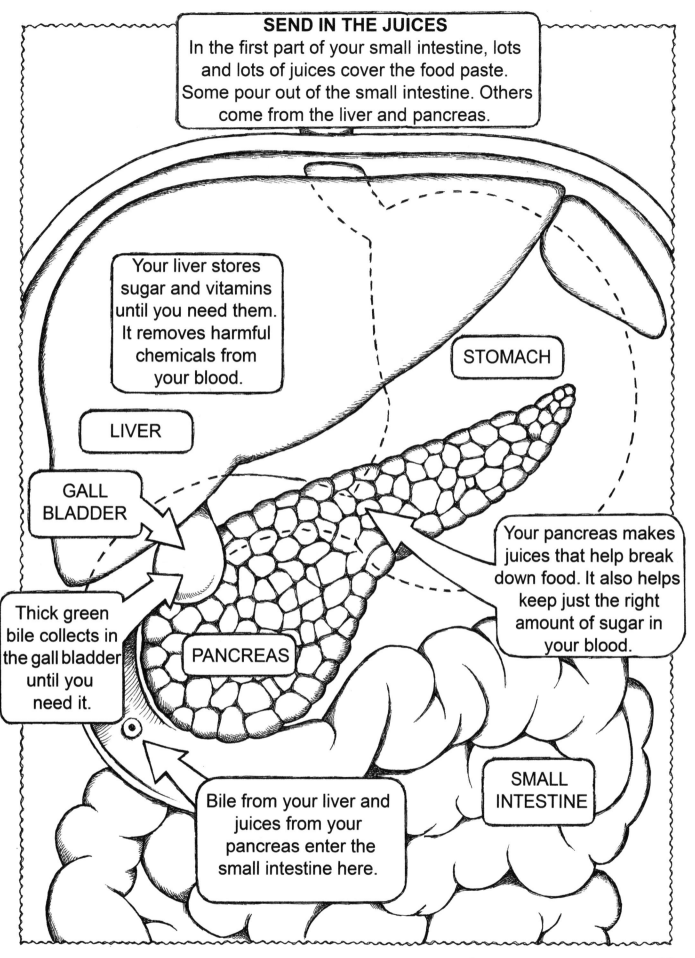

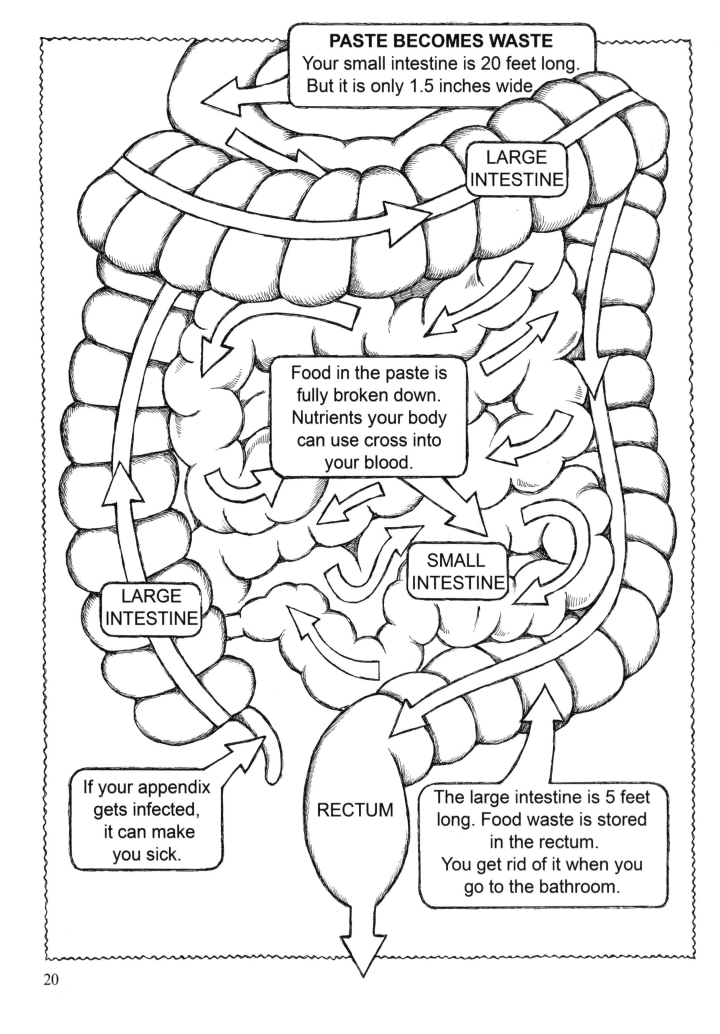

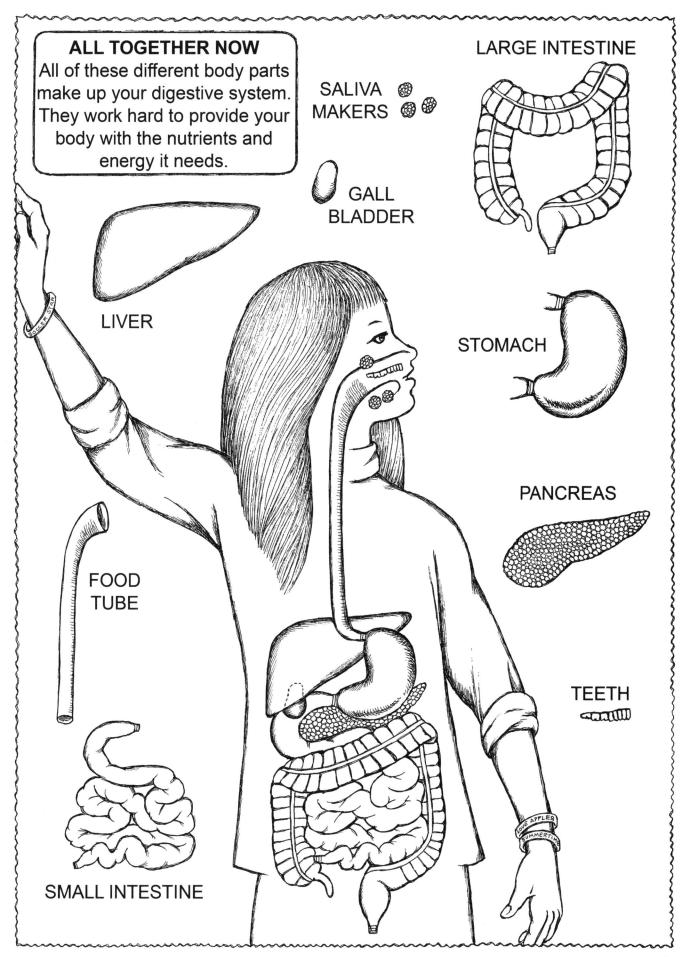

ALL TOGETHER NOW
All of these different body parts make up your digestive system. They work hard to provide your body with the nutrients and energy it needs.

SALIVA MAKERS

GALL BLADDER

LARGE INTESTINE

LIVER

STOMACH

PANCREAS

FOOD TUBE

TEETH

SMALL INTESTINE

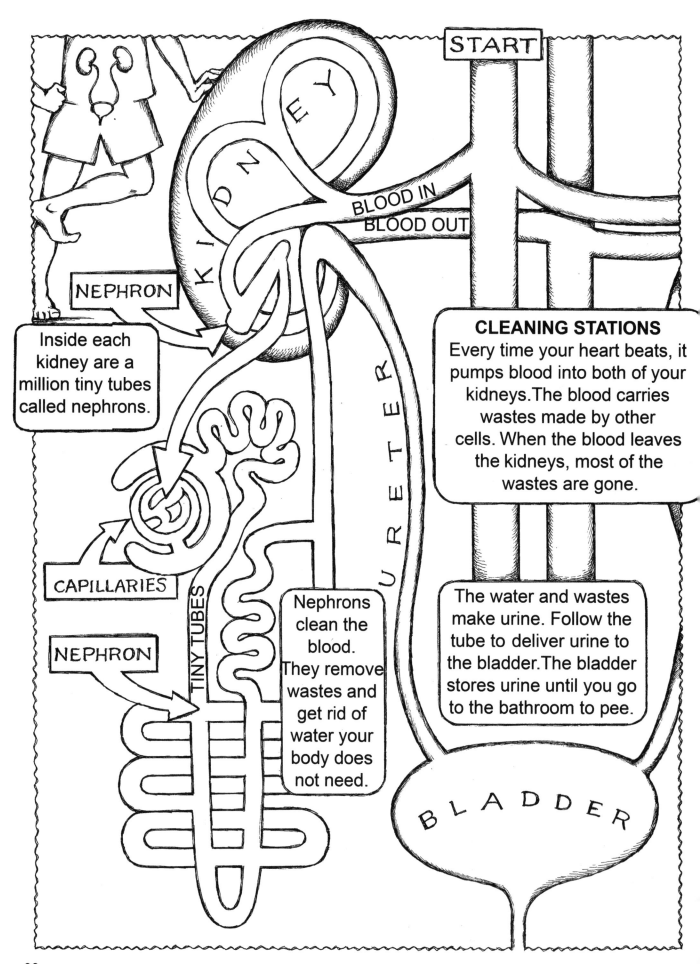

START

KIDNEY

BLOOD IN
BLOOD OUT

NEPHRON

Inside each kidney are a million tiny tubes called nephrons.

CAPILLARIES

NEPHRON

TINY TUBES

URETER

CLEANING STATIONS
Every time your heart beats, it pumps blood into both of your kidneys. The blood carries wastes made by other cells. When the blood leaves the kidneys, most of the wastes are gone.

Nephrons clean the blood. They remove wastes and get rid of water your body does not need.

The water and wastes make urine. Follow the tube to deliver urine to the bladder. The bladder stores urine until you go to the bathroom to pee.

BLADDER

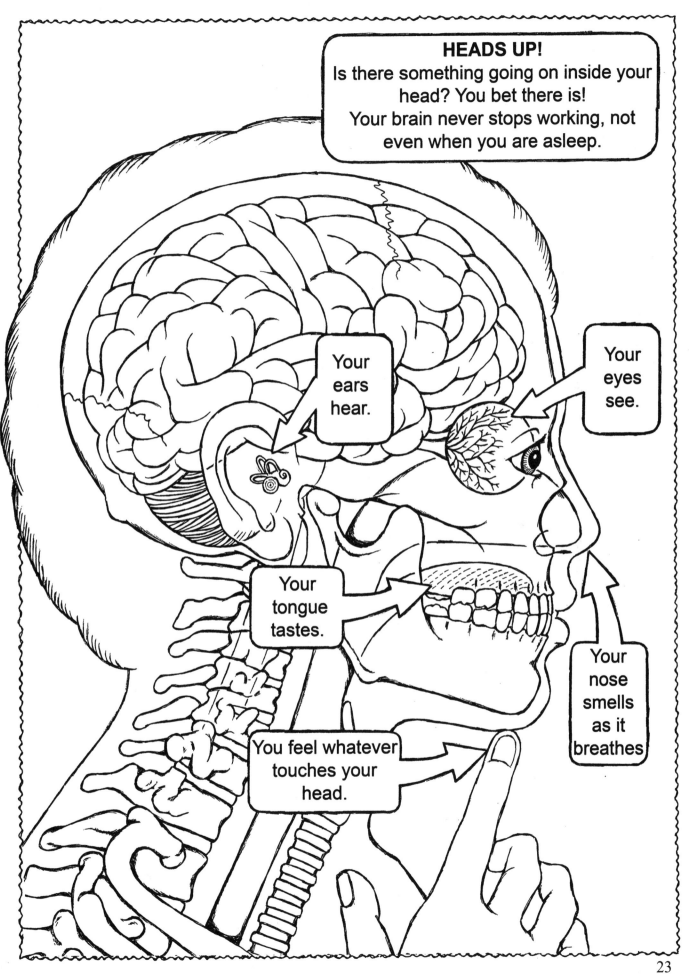

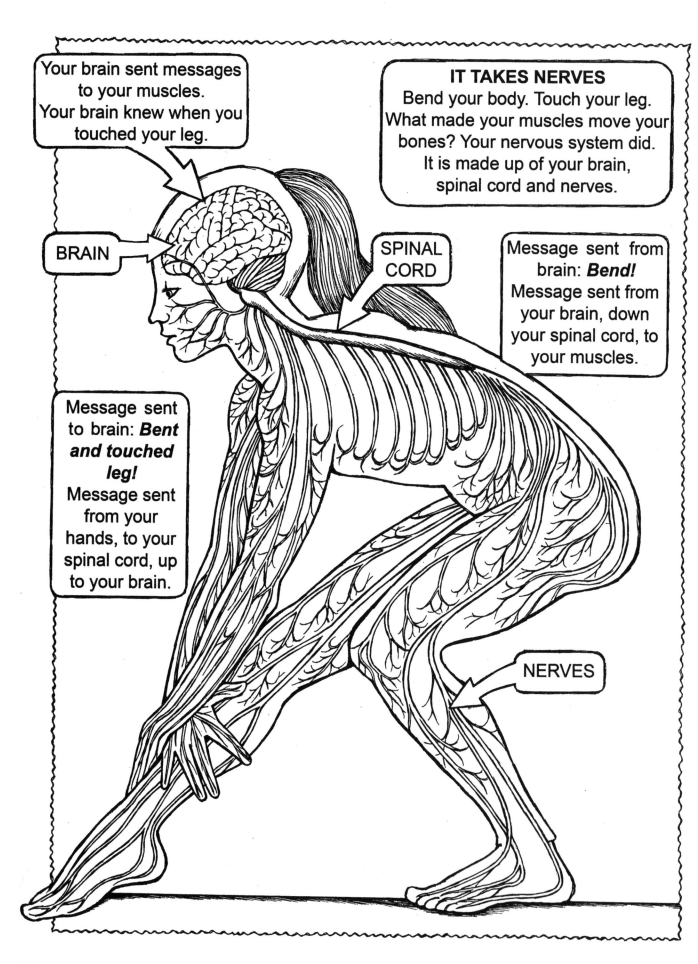

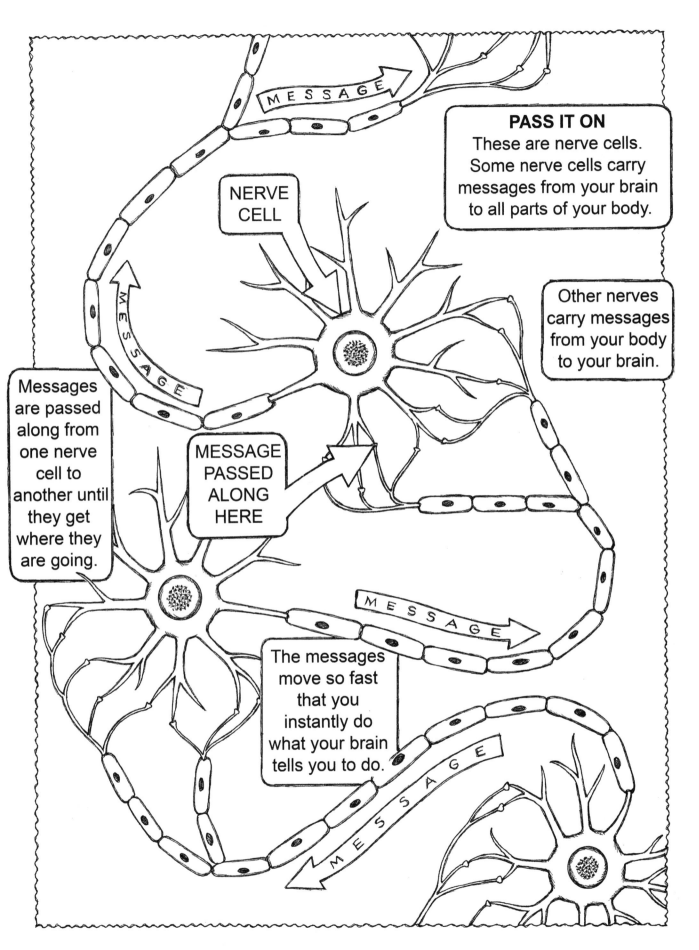

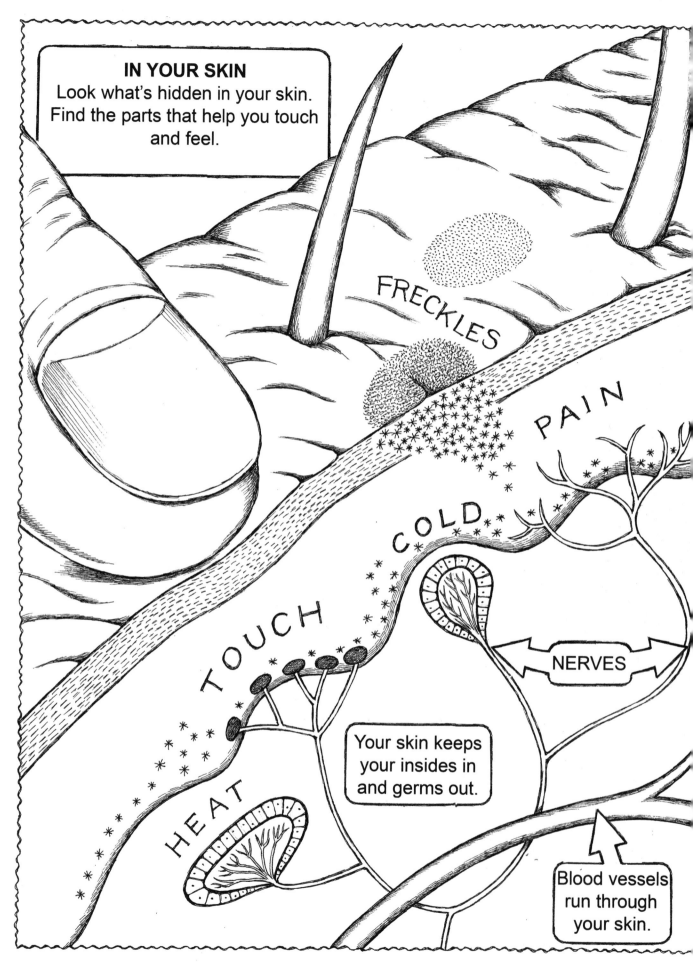

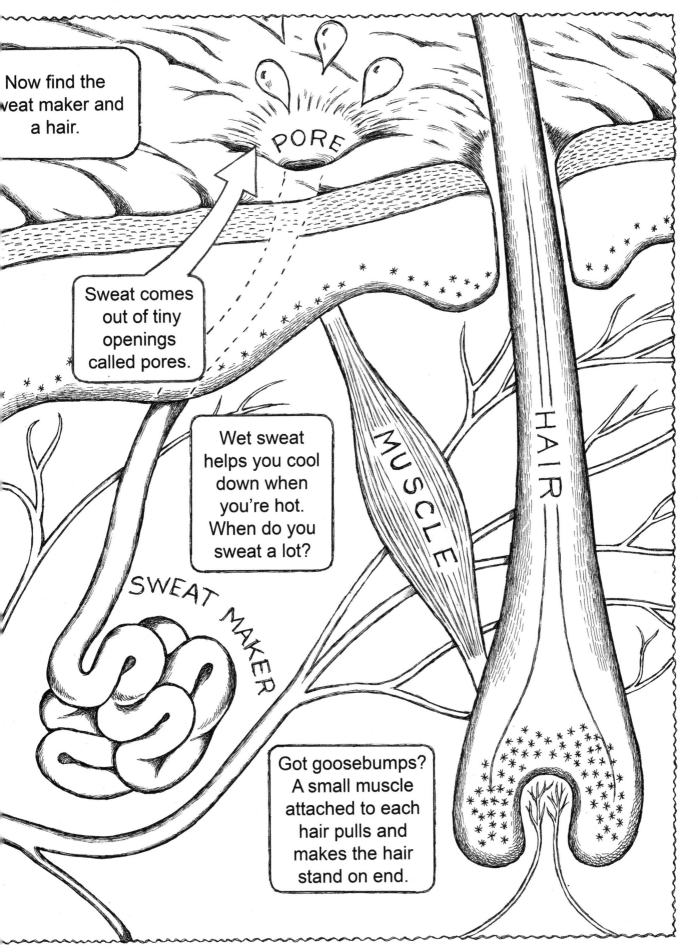

27

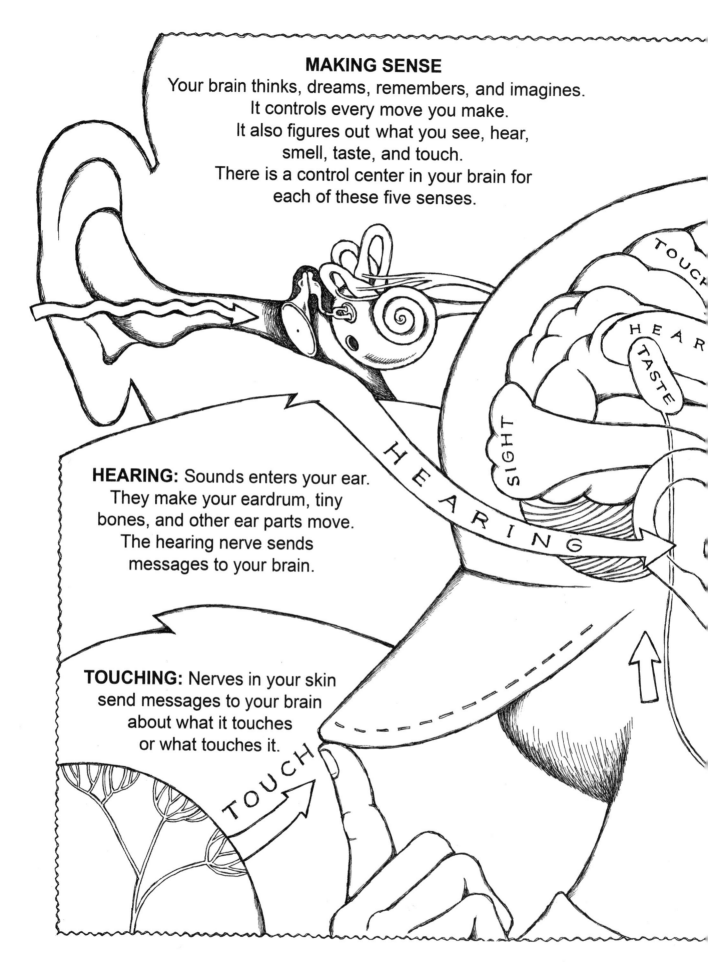

MAKING SENSE
Your brain thinks, dreams, remembers, and imagines.
It controls every move you make.
It also figures out what you see, hear,
smell, taste, and touch.
There is a control center in your brain for
each of these five senses.

TOUCH

HEAR

TASTE

SIGHT

HEARING

HEARING: Sounds enters your ear.
They make your eardrum, tiny
bones, and other ear parts move.
The hearing nerve sends
messages to your brain.

TOUCHING: Nerves in your skin
send messages to your brain
about what it touches
or what touches it.

TOUCH

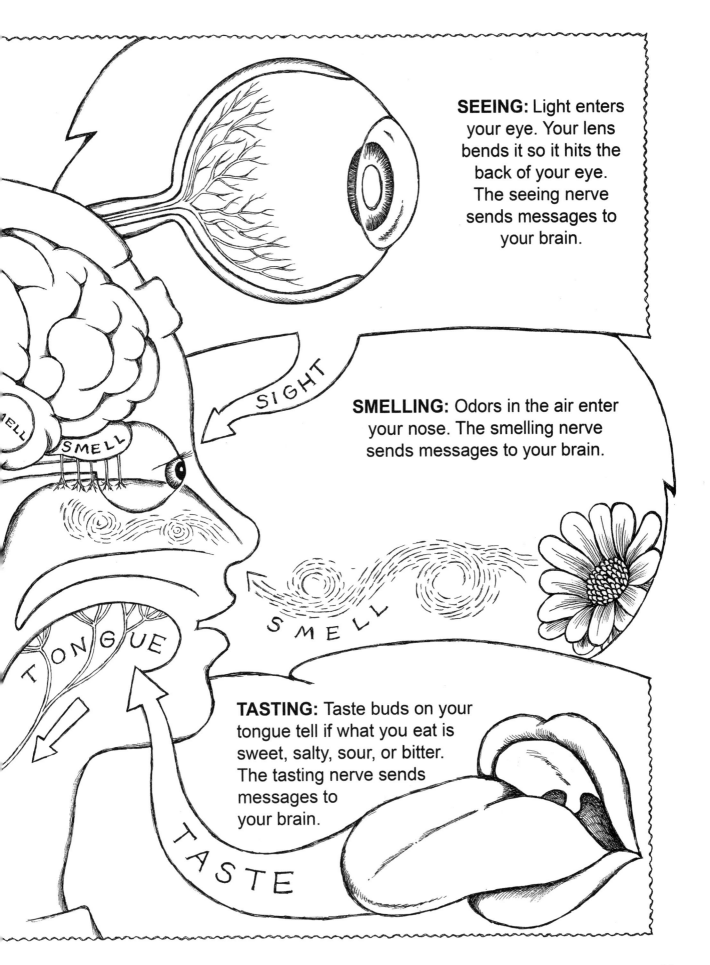

SEEING: Light enters your eye. Your lens bends it so it hits the back of your eye. The seeing nerve sends messages to your brain.

SMELLING: Odors in the air enter your nose. The smelling nerve sends messages to your brain.

TASTING: Taste buds on your tongue tell if what you eat is sweet, salty, sour, or bitter. The tasting nerve sends messages to your brain.

SIGHT

SMELL

SMELL

TONGUE

TASTE

29

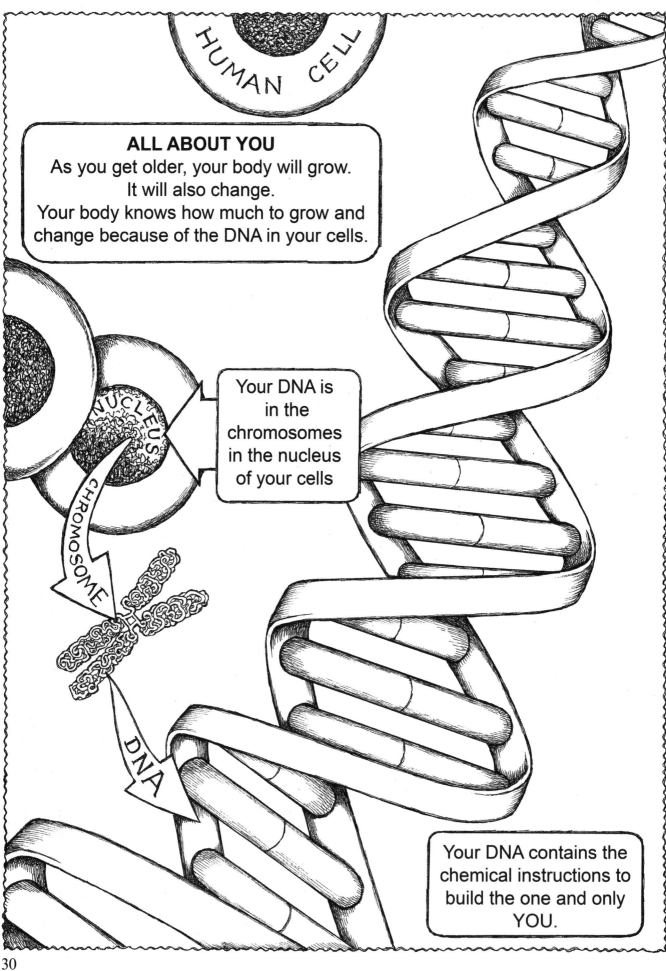

ALL ABOUT YOU
As you get older, your body will grow.
It will also change.
Your body knows how much to grow and
change because of the DNA in your cells.

Your DNA is in the chromosomes in the nucleus of your cells

HUMAN CELL

NUCLEUS

CHROMOSOME

DNA

Your DNA contains the chemical instructions to build the one and only YOU.